TIME TO COMPARE

Which HOLDS MORE?

BY JAGGER YOUSSEF

Gareth Stevens
PUBLISHING

first concepts

We can compare!
The big mug
holds more.

TIME TO COMPARE!

Which HOLDS MORE?

JAGGER YOUSSEF

first concepts

3

The purple cup
holds more.

5

The white can
holds more.

7

The yellow spoon holds more.

9

The orange box
holds more.

11

The bathtub
holds more.

13

The red pot
holds more.

15

The milk jug
holds more.

17

The right bucket
holds more.

19

The left bottle
holds more.

21

Point to the fish bowl
that holds more.

23

Please visit our website, www.garethstevens.com. For a free color catalog of all our high-quality books, call toll free 1-800-542-2595 or fax 1-877-542-2596.

Library of Congress Cataloging-in-Publication Data
Names: Youssef, Jagger, author.
Title: Which holds more? / Jagger Youssef.
Description: New York : Gareth Stevens Publishing, [2021] | Series: Time to compare! | Includes index.
Identifiers: LCCN 2019042311 | ISBN 9781538255209 (library binding) | ISBN 9781538255186 (paperback) | ISBN 9781538255193 | ISBN 9781538255216 (ebook)
Subjects: LCSH: Volume (Cubic content)–Juvenile literature. | Volume perception–Juvenile literature. | Comparison (Psychology) in children–Juvenile literature.
Classification: LCC QC104 .Y68 2021 | DDC 530.8–dc23
LC record available at https://lccn.loc.gov/2019042311

First Edition

Published in 2021 by
Gareth Stevens Publishing
111 East 14th Street, Suite 349
New York, NY 10003

Copyright © 2021 Gareth Stevens Publishing

Designer: Sarah Liddell
Editor: Therese Shea

Photo credits: Cover, p. 1 (main) Alter-ego/Shutterstock.com; cover, p. 1 (background) oksanka007/Shutterstock.com; p. 3 (left) robertsre/Shutterstock.com; p. 3 (right) New Africa/Shutterstock.com; p. 5 JIANG HONGYAN/Shutterstock.com; p. 7 (left) Brooke Becker/Shutterstock.com; p. 7 (right) Christian Delbert/Shutterstock.com; p. 9 Aleksandr Pobedimskiy/Shutterstock.com; p. 11 (left) Africa Studio/Shutterstock.com; p. 11 (right) Lovely Bird/Shutterstock.com; p. 13 (top) Danny Smythe/Shutterstock.com; p. 13 (bottom) Ttatty/Shutterstock.com; p. 15 (top) Purple Moon/Shutterstock.com; p. 15 (bottom) Jiri Hera/Shutterstock.com; p. 17 (left) Photo Melon/Shutterstock.com; p. 17 (right) Andrey_Kuzmin/Shutterstock.com; p. 19 (left) Timmary/Shutterstock.com; p. 19 (right) mylisa/Shutterstock.com; p. 21 givaga/Shutterstock.com; p. 23 r.classen/Shutterstock.com.

Printed in the United States of America

Some of the images in this book illustrate individuals who are models. The depictions do not imply actual situations or events.

CPSIA compliance information: Batch #CS20GS: For further information contact Gareth Stevens, New York, New York at 1-800-542-2595.

Find us on